The Wellness
ACTIVITY BOOK

An Approach to Preserving Families
and Relationships

Camella Jones MBS, LPC-Intern

Order this book online at www.trafford.com
or email orders@trafford.com

Most Trafford titles are also available at major online book retailers.

Printed in the United States of America.

ISBN: 978-1-4269-6162-5 (sc)
ISBN: 978-1-4269-6185-4 (e)

Trafford rev. 11/15/2011

www.trafford.com

North America & International
toll-free: 1 888 232 4444 (USA & Canada)
phone: 250 383 6864 ♦ fax: 812 355 4082

Acknowledgements

Nurse Holly,

Thanks for challenging me to develop a unique way to improve our health and wellness

A very special thank you to my Husband, Leon, and my four sons: Miles, Timothy, Vance and Kennedy. Our special family meetings have drawn Us closer and become a safe environment To share our inner most feelings. I love you.

Deepest thanks to my Lord and Savior, Jesus Christ.

The Wellness Activity book

If you want to move toward a better state of wellness in many aspects of your life, The Wellness Activity book is just what you need. But first, let's spend just a moment to explore the picture of wellness. First, when most people think of wellness, they think of physical acts such as exercise and dieting. Simply put, wellness equals weight loss for most people. However, wellness encompasses so much more. For example, wellness entails many of the things we do that help us feel whole and purposeful: things like reaching a personal goal, establishing boundaries in our world, and finding creative ways to solve problems in our lives, as well as the lives of others. To think even broader, it's giving ourselves credit for taking an extra step when our legs are telling us to sit down. Wellness is encouraging others to make better choices that will ultimately form better habits. It's smiling rather than frowning over the daily pressures of life, to do more and more with what seems like less and less time to get it all done. To me, wellness is about keeping yourself number one on the priority list and ensuring that your own sense of wellness is examined routinely.

When we focus on wellness, we begin developing habits that encourage us to make better choices that we hope will result in an improved quality of life. The result of such improvements will manifest itself into a revamped individual who is able to function better psychologically, socially, emotionally and even spiritually.

If you are anything like me, you have tried multiple diets and have experienced many moments of success. However, you probably discovered that when it is all said and done you're left with an ultimate sense of failure after the weight quietly creeps back upon you. I believe the biggest challenge in keeping your weight off is your tendency to shift your entire focus on your outer appearance, which is what is often used to gauge your success. Too often you give yourself no credit at all for the true effort that is required to attain even the smallest weight loss goal. Often times when you start a diet you push your friends and family to the side because they are not on the same "diet wave length." Do you find it ironic that you are pushing away these people during a time you could use their support the most?

I have found this to be true in my own life, as well as with thousands of women I have coached to become more healthy throughout my career. Each of these women seemed to share an ability to get off to a great dieting start only to gradually fizzle out. It is unfortunate that children and the elderly are experiencing this same frustration as they strive to reach and maintain an ideal level of wellness.

Though the diet blast off is exciting at first, I am certain many people are tired of the crash landing and temporary results. It is my belief that the crash landing occurs because of inner turmoil or frustration that gets in the way of our focus. It is not until you deliberately acknowledge many of the good choices you make that contribute to your wellness will you deliberately continue to make the choices that are able to make you well. Confronting poor choices, addressing unresolved baggage, and allowing for an escape from the tough demands of daily life can help you begin to feel better about yourself and move toward a greater level of life satisfaction and long-lasting success.

The Wellness Activity book will teach you how to credit yourself for the positive choices you make that contribute toward your wellness but are not directly related to weight loss. The outlined activities are designed to make others feel good as a result of your actions. It is wellness made simple and fun and will inspire you to do something out of the ordinary that will lead to a sense of pride and inner peace. The Wellness Activity book allows you to track your wellness on a daily basis and extends an invitation to friends and other supporters to join in so that everyone is a winner.

Tracking your progress is simple because the challenge is based on an honor system. Your ongoing results can either be for your eyes only, or it can be shared with others. However, it should be decided up front if the team chooses to have an open book, whereby results are shared at least weekly. Each challenger should weigh both at the beginning and end of the challenge. It is recommended that each participant weigh on the same day of the week and on the same scale if at all possible.

Challengers are encouraged to get familiar with the categories and then tally all points at the end of the day. Ideally, the challenge last for four weeks and offers a grand prize for the winner (or winning team). Prize ideas can include splitting the pot for all entry fees collected/ Also, participants may work to win an incentive prize that would be appealing to all contestants, or the entire group of challengers or pairs of challengers may enjoy a fun party in the end. The challenge is so simple it can be done between children, family members, co-workers, and church peers. Parents can challenge their children to move toward a better state of wellness or husbands can challenge their wives. Get the picture? There's no wrong way to inspire someone else to make healthier choices.

Use the daily points guide in the back of the book to tally your points and keep a running total throughout the designated challenge days. Establish criterion for the challenge such as entry fees and incentives. Define any new categories and assess point values early on to ensure all team members are aware of qualifying actions. Keep a running tally of your points each day and calculate your grand total at the end of the challenge. Remember, if you are on a team, each member will combine their points for a grand total. Make it fun by naming your team and publicizing weekly points with colorful banners or posters. Or you can torment your opponents by keeping your points a secret until the end of the challenge!

As you look at the Daily Point Reference Guide you will see that the focus of The Wellness Activity book is not weight loss. However, you are likely going to experience weight loss as a result of your good choices, and I certainly want to applaud your efforts. So, for every pound you lose during the challenge add a point to your grand total.

I have assessed a point value for each category. However, there are countless categories you may wish to add to make your challenge more individualized. As I mentioned before, it is imperative that you assess a point value for any new categories adopted into the challenge and use the blank lines for this purpose. The team or individual with the most points wins the challenge. It's that simple. In the event of a tie, feel free to extend the challenge an additional week. Oh yes, before I forget: be sure to consult your doctor before beginning this program and adhere to any precautions or modifications recommended. Have fun!!!

Daily Point Reference Guide

Physical and Nutritional Health Category—20 point value

Starting your day with a healthy breakfast

Taking your medications as prescribed daily

Engaging in any type of exercise for 20 minutes (add 10 pts. for each additional 10 minutes)

Consuming 8 oz. water (add 10 points for each additional 8 oz. glass)

Consuming a daily vitamin or nutritional supplement

Engaging in a full body stretch routine of your choice for at least 10 minutes

Consuming a piece of fruit (add 10 pts. for each additional fruit serving each day)

Consuming a vegetable (add 10 pts. for each additional vegetable serving each day)

Completing a wellness check-up by your doctor

Getting eight hours of sleep

_____

_____

_____

_____

_____

_____

Spiritual Category—20 point value

Talking to a trusted friend about a problem
Seeking professional counsel for a problem
Attending a church or religious function
Visiting a homebound, jailed or hospitalized individual
Praying, meditating, or reading a spiritual work
Listening to a spiritual message
Tithing or making a special financial contribution to a church or charitable organization
Starting a conversation about God
Telling someone about Christ
Telling someone you love them (1 pt. for each additional occurrence)
Consoling someone after a loss or disappointment
Giving someone a compliment (1 pt. for each additional occurrence)

_____

_____

_____

_____

_____

_____

_____

Altruistic Category—20 point value

Encouraging a team mate or opponent during the challenge

Performing a heroic act

Contacting someone you haven't spoken to in at least six months

Volunteering your service for a charitable cause

Making a financial contribution to a non-profit organization

Showing a random act of kindness

Reading a book together as a family

Hosting a spa night for your family

Tutoring someone in any area

Facilitating a bible study at work

Having a bible study with your family

Buying dinner for a friend or someone less fortunate

Interviewing an elderly family member and sharing the responses with extended family

Adopting a pet

Adopting a grand parent

Teaching someone a skill or trade that you have mastered

Donating blood, tissue or organs

_____

_____

_____

_____

_____

_____

Personal Enrichment Category—20 point value

Taking a first step toward a personal goal (enrolling in an educational course)

Reading a self enrichment book

Giving someone a hug

Giving someone a nurturing touch

Giving a well-deserved apology

Saying to someone, "I love you" (1 pt. for each additional instance)

Gardening or lawn care to relieve stress and enhance relaxation

Spending time with your pets

Telling yourself "I love you"

Searching for an old friend

Discovering a new hobby and incorporating it into your regular routine

Quitting an unhealthy habit, i.e. smoking, drinking, overeating at meal time

Discovering a solution to problem

Laughing hysterically at something funny

Telling an appropriate joke (1 pt. for each additional instance)

Doing anything for yourself that enhances your self esteem

Trying a new food

Preparing a new recipe

Having a spiritual moment with your family

Giving someone you love a massage

Sharing a personal goal, dream or fantasy with a friend

Informing someone about The Wellness Activity Book

Taking an Activity Wellness survey
Establish a family budget
Pledge to become debt free and seek financial counsel

_____

_____

_____

_____

_____

_____

_____

_____

_____

Relaxation Category—25 point value

Taking time out of your day to read
Engaging in any relaxing activity for 30 minutes (i.e., listening to music,)
Listening to a motivating message
Window shopping
Taking a vacation
Spending one hour of uninterrupted time with someone else doing some thing fun
Gardening
Spending time with your pet
Taking a relaxing bath
Getting a massage or pampering yourself in some way
Taking a day off work to relax
Taking a scenic drive or ride
Turning off your cell phone for the evening
Going on a nature walk
Engaging in an art or craft activity
Playing a game with your child or spouse

_____

_____

_____

_____

_____

Additional points ideas for children—25 point value

Baking cookies for someone
Making good marks on a report card
Receiving a special award or recognition at school
Painting or coloring a picture for someone to admire
Turning off the television for the evening
Going on a bike ride with a parent
Saying a daily prayer with or for a family member
Reading the bible or a devotional
Cleaning your room without being reminded
Reading a book about something you would like to know about
Tutoring a friend that needs help
Putting together a puzzle
Talking to your parents about your day
Putting away your cell phone or electronic game for the evening
Performing a community service
Spending quality time with your pet
Enjoying a bubble bath
Doing a good deed for your sibling
Choosing to go outside to play with friends instead of staying indoors
Taking the parent survey
Starting an indoor garden
Listening to a funny story told by a senior adult

_____

_____

_____

Take the Survey

Have you ever wondered how your friends would rate your friendship if you were to give them a friendship survey? Well, how about your kids, spouse, or significant other? How would they view your loyalty and devotion? By participating in any of these brief surveys, you can gain an idea of how others perceive you. Hopefully the feedback you receive will help you gain insight as you self examine. Feel free to conduct any of these surveys during any given week as long as you do not give them to the same individuals during a designated challenge. It is perfectly fine to re-survey the same individuals in subsequent challenges to see if your rating increases as a result of their feedback.

I encourage you to survey as many of your friends in a given week in order to learn more about possible changes that can be made to improve the quality of your relationships. Learning how others perceive you can be valuable in the development of character and learning to become a better you. Should you find the results of any of these surveys disturbing, please consult a counselor to assist you in processing your feelings. Developing an ability to grow from the feedback from others is a positive sign of wellness.

I predict that parents surveying their children will gain insight from responses received. For those parents with multiple children be sure to survey each child. Children taking the challenge can survey their parents or caregivers and also add the points to their weekly total. I encourage parents to take the results of the survey taken by your child to heart. Knowing how your child views your relationship is priceless. It is also a perfect invitation to begin a family routine that welcomes structure and quality family time.

Learning to balance work, family, community and social activities can be a juggling act. Let your child make it simple for you by allowing them to share their ideas and suggestions on how to incorporate them into your busy world.

Parents taking the child survey are encouraged to sit down with their child and discuss the results. This is a good practice because each individual in the relationship knows where they stand and has an opportunity to work on any problems that have been identified. This discussion will be especially valuable to your child as you discuss the results of the child survey taken by the parent. I have included extra surveys in each area to allow for re-evaluations. I believe you will find your efforts to be worthwhile and a sure way to open the door of communication as you move toward improving the quality of your relationships.

The spiritual survey is designed to help you examine your faith and spiritual character. After all, it's our spirituality that moves us to shift the focus from our own problems and needs to the concerns of others, right? It's a private matter and is included to encourage you to take a brief moment to assess this area of your life to determine if any improvements are warranted.

This is how the surveys work. Ask a friend, spouse, or child to rate you on a point scale from 1 to 5 with one being the least score possible to five being the greatest score possible on each item. Keep up with the points and tally them at the end of the survey. For example, the friendship survey has six items.

Suppose you are rated the following points on each item: Item 1 = 3 points Item 2 = 4 points Item 3= 2 points Item 4= 5 points and item 6= 4 points. Your total points for that survey is 18. Simply add 18 points to your daily total. You may survey as many friends as you desire throughout the challenge. All surveys are scored similarly.

Friendship Survey

I spend quality time with my friend doing things that make us laugh and relax

1   2   3   4   5

I make my friend feel important by calling, visiting or using other forms of communication

1   2   3   4   5

I am there for my friend during both happy and difficult times

1   2   3   4   5

I am willing to apologize to my friend when I am wrong. I am also willing to gently confront my friend when I feel they are in need of redirection

1   2   3   4   5

I am quick to notice subtle changes in my friend related to their appearance, personality, attitude, etc.

1   2   3   4   5

My friend perceives me as a positive influence the majority of the time

1   2   3   4   5

Friendship Survey

I spend quality time with my friend doing things that make us laugh and relax

1   **2**   **3**   **4**   **5**

I make my friend feel important by calling, visiting or using other forms of communication

1   **2**   **3**   **4**   **5**

I am there for my friend during both happy and difficult times

1   **2**   **3**   **4**   **5**

I am willing to apologize to my friend when I am wrong. I am also willing to gently confront my friend when I feel they are in need of redirection

1   **2**   **3**   **4**   **5**

I am quick to notice subtle changes in my friend related to their appearance, personality, attitude, etc.

1   **2**   **3**   **4**   **5**

My friend perceives me as a positive influence the majority of the time

1   **2**   **3**   **4**   **5**

Friendship Survey

I spend quality time with my friend doing things that make us laugh and relax

1   2   3   4   5

I make my friend feel important by calling, visiting or using other forms of communication

1   2   3   4   5

I am there for my friend during both happy and difficult times

1   2   3   4   5

I am willing to apologize to my friend when I am wrong. I am also willing to gently confront my friend when I feel they are in need of redirection

1   2   3   4   5

I am quick to notice subtle changes in my friend related to their appearance, personality, attitude, etc.

1   2   3   4   5

My friend perceives me as a positive influence the majority of the time

1   2   3   4   5

Friendship Survey

I spend quality time with my friend doing things that make us laugh and relax

1   2   3   4   5

I make my friend feel important by calling, visiting or using other forms of communication

1   2   3   4   5

I am there for my friend during both happy and difficult times

1   2   3   4   5

I am willing to apologize to my friend when I am wrong. I am also willing to gently confront my friend when I feel they are in need of redirection

1   2   3   4   5

I am quick to notice subtle changes in my friend related to their appearance, personality, attitude, etc.

1   2   3   4   5

My friend perceives me as a positive influence the majority of the time

1   2   3   4   5

Friendship Survey

I spend quality time with my friend doing things that make us laugh and relax

1   2   3   4   5

I make my friend feel important by calling, visiting or using other forms of communication

1   2   3   4   5

I am there for my friend during both happy and difficult times

1   2   3   4   5

I am willing to apologize to my friend when I am wrong. I am also willing to gently confront my friend when I feel they are in need of redirection

1   2   3   4   5

I am quick to notice subtle changes in my friend related to their appearance, personality, attitude, etc.

1   2   3   4   5

My friend perceives me as a positive influence the majority of the time

1   2   3   4   5

Friendship Survey

I spend quality time with my friend doing things that make us laugh and relax

1   2   3   4   5

I make my friend feel important by calling, visiting or using other forms of communication

1   2   3   4   5

I am there for my friend during both happy and difficult times

1   2   3   4   5

I am willing to apologize to my friend when I am wrong. I am also willing to gently confront my friend when I feel they are in need of redirection

1   2   3   4   5

I am quick to notice subtle changes in my friend related to their appearance, personality, attitude, etc.

1   2   3   4   5

My friend perceives me as a positive influence the majority of the time

1   2   3   4   5

Parent Survey to be taken by child

My parent(s) spend quality time with me each day doing things that I enjoy

1   2   3   4   5

My parents compliment me. Their encouragement contributes to my healthy self esteem

1   2   3   4   5

I feel comfortable talking to my parents about sensitive topics such as drugs, sex, bullies, etc.

1   2   3   4   5

I feel my parents support my interest and or extra curricular activities

1   2   3   4   5

I know what makes my parents proud of me and what disappoints them

1   2   3   4   5

I know a funny childhood story about my parents past

1   2   3   4   5

Camella Jones

My parents do not allow distractions such as television, work, or cell phones to interfere with time meant for me

1   2   3   4   5

I feel my parents are fair with their consequences and discipline me out of love

1   2   3   4   5

Parent Survey to be taken by child

My parent(s) spend quality time with me each day doing things that I enjoy

1   2   3   4   5

My parents compliment me. Their encouragement contributes to my healthy self esteem

1   2   3   4   5

I feel comfortable talking to my parents about sensitive topics such as drugs, sex, bullies, etc.

1   2   3   4   5

I feel my parents support my interest and or extra curricular activities

1   2   3   4   5

I know what makes my parents proud of me and what disappoints them

1   2   3   4   5

I know a funny childhood story about my parents past

1   2   3   4   5

My parents do not allow distractions such as television, work, or cell phones to interfere with time meant for me

1   2   3   4   5

I feel my parents are fair with their consequences and discipline me out of love

1   2   3   4   5

Parent Survey to be taken by child

My parent(s) spend quality time with me each day doing things that I enjoy

1   2   3   4   5

My parents compliment me. Their encouragement contributes to my healthy self esteem

1   2   3   4   5

I feel comfortable talking to my parents about sensitive topics such as drugs, sex, bullies, etc.

1   2   3   4   5

I feel my parents support my interest and or extra curricular activities

1   2   3   4   5

I know what makes my parents proud of me and what disappoints them

1   2   3   4   5

I know a funny childhood story about my parents past

1   2   3   4   5

Camella Jones

My parents do not allow distractions such as television, work, or cell phones to interfere with time meant for me

1   2   3   4   5

I feel my parents are fair with their consequences and discipline me out of love

1   2   3   4   5

Parent Survey to be taken by child

My parent(s) spend quality time with me each day doing things that I enjoy

1   2   3   4   5

My parents compliment me. Their encouragement contributes to my healthy self esteem

1   2   3   4   5

I feel comfortable talking to my parents about sensitive topics such as drugs, sex, bullies, etc.

1   2   3   4   5

I feel my parents support my interest and or extra curricular activities

1   2   3   4   5

I know what makes my parents proud of me and what disappoints them

1   2   3   4   5

I know a funny childhood story about my parents past

1   2   3   4   5

My parents do not allow distractions such as television, work, or cell phones to interfere with time meant for me

1   2   3   4   5

I feel my parents are fair with their consequences and discipline me out of love

1   2   3   4   5

Parent Survey to be taken by child

My parent(s) spend quality time with me each day doing things that I enjoy

1   2   3   4   5

My parents compliment me. Their encouragement contributes to my healthy self esteem

1   2   3   4   5

I feel comfortable talking to my parents about sensitive topics such as drugs, sex, bullies, etc.

1   2   3   4   5

I feel my parents support my interest and or extra curricular activities

1   2   3   4   5

I know what makes my parents proud of me and what disappoints them

1   2   3   4   5

I know a funny childhood story about my parents past

1   2   3   4   5

My parents do not allow distractions such as television, work, or cell phones to interfere with time meant for me

1   2   3   4   5

I feel my parents are fair with their consequences and discipline me out of love

1   2   3   4   5

Parent Survey to be taken by child

My parent(s) spend quality time with me each day doing things that I enjoy

1   2   3   4   5

My parents compliment me. Their encouragement contributes to my healthy self esteem

1   2   3   4   5

I feel comfortable talking to my parents about sensitive topics such as drugs, sex, bullies, etc.

1   2   3   4   5

I feel my parents support my interest and or extra curricular activities

1   2   3   4   5

I know what makes my parents proud of me and what disappoints them

1   2   3   4   5

I know a funny childhood story about my parents past

1   2   3   4   5

Camella Jones

My parents do not allow distractions such as television, work, or cell phones to interfere with time meant for me

1   2   3   4   5

I feel my parents are fair with their consequences and discipline me out of love

1   2   3   4   5

Child Survey to be taken by parents

I know my child is making their best effort in school

1   2   3   4   5

I can depend on my child to follow through on commitments

1   2   3   4   5

My child shows initiative to do things that need to be done without having to be told

1   2   3   4   5

My child talks to me when they have a problem or a concern. I pray with and for my child

1   2   3   4   5

My child is focused and is on the right track

1   2   3   4   5

My child is accountable for his behavior and is willing to apologize when needed

1   2   3   4   5

I know what my child wants to be when he grows up

1   2   3   4   5

My child belongs to a positive youth group that instills good values and teachings

1   2   3   4   5

My child has a positive male role model in his life who makes them feel valued, encouraged and appreciated

1   2   3   4   5

My child has received counsel for any traumatic event or loss in order to process their feelings

1   2   3   4   5

Child Survey to be taken by parents

I know my child is making their best effort in school

1   2   3   4   5

I can depend on my child to follow through on commitments

1   2   3   4   5

My child shows initiative to do things that need to be done without having to be told

1   2   3   4   5

My child talks to me when they have a problem or a concern. I pray with and for my child

1   2   3   4   5

My child is focused and is on the right track

1   2   3   4   5

My child is accountable for his behavior and is willing to apologize when needed

1   2   3   4   5

I know what my child wants to be when he grows up

1   2   3   4   5

My child belongs to a positive youth group that instills good values and teachings

1   2   3   4   5

My child has a positive male role model in his life who makes them feel valued, encouraged and appreciated

1   2   3   4   5

My child has received counsel for any traumatic event or loss in order to process their feelings

1   2   3   4   5

Child Survey to be taken by parents

I know my child is making their best effort in school

1   2   3   4   5

I can depend on my child to follow through on commitments

1   2   3   4   5

My child shows initiative to do things that need to be done without having to be told

1   2   3   4   5

My child talks to me when they have a problem or a concern. I pray with and for my child

1   2   3   4   5

My child is focused and is on the right track

1   2   3   4   5

My child is accountable for his behavior and is willing to apologize when needed

1   2   3   4   5

I know what my child wants to be when he grows up

1   2   3   4   5

My child belongs to a positive youth group that instills good values and teachings

1   2   3   4   5

My child has a positive male role model in his life who makes them feel valued, encouraged and appreciated

1   2   3   4   5

My child has received counsel for any traumatic event or loss in order to process their feelings

1   2   3   4   5

Child Survey to be taken by parents

I know my child is making their best effort in school

1   2   3   4   5

I can depend on my child to follow through on commitments

1   2   3   4   5

My child shows initiative to do things that need to be done without having to be told

1   2   3   4   5

My child talks to me when they have a problem or a concern. I pray with and for my child

1   2   3   4   5

My child is focused and is on the right track

1   2   3   4   5

My child is accountable for his behavior and is willing to apologize when needed

1   2   3   4   5

I know what my child wants to be when he grows up

1   2   3   4   5

My child belongs to a positive youth group that instills good values and teachings

1   2   3   4   5

My child has a positive male role model in his life who makes them feel valued, encouraged and appreciated

1   2   3   4   5

My child has received counsel for any traumatic event or loss in order to process their feelings

1   2   3   4   5

Child Survey to be taken by parents

I know my child is making their best effort in school

1   2   3   4   5

I can depend on my child to follow through on commitments

1   2   3   4   5

My child shows initiative to do things that need to be done without having to be told

1   2   3   4   5

My child talks to me when they have a problem or a concern, I pray with and for my child

1   2   3   4   5

My child is focused and is on the right track

1   2   3   4   5

My child is accountable for his behavior and is willing to apologize when needed

1   2   3   4   5

I know what my child wants to be when he grows up

1   2   3   4   5

My child belongs to a positive youth group that instills good values and teachings

1   2   3   4   5

My child has a positive male role model in his life who makes them feel valued, encouraged and appreciated

1   2   3   4   5

My child has received counsel for any traumatic event or loss in order to process their feelings

1   2   3   4   5

Child Survey to be taken by parents

I know my child is making their best effort in school

1   2   3   4   5

I can depend on my child to follow through on commitments

1   2   3   4   5

My child shows initiative to do things that need to be done without having to be told

1   2   3   4   5

My child talks to me when they have a problem or a concern

1   2   3   4   5

My child is focused and is on the right track

1   2   3   4   5

My child is accountable for his behavior and is willing to apologize when needed

1   2   3   4   5

I know what my child wants to be when he grows up

1   2   3   4   5

My child belongs to a positive youth group that instills good values and teachings

1   2   3   4   5

My child has a positive male role model in his life who makes them feel valued, encouraged and appreciated

1   2   3   4   5

My child has received counsel for any traumatic event or loss in order to process their feelings

1   2   3   4   5

Spirituality

Exercising positive social behaviors and attitudes can attribute to a great sense of spiritual wellness that can result in creative activities benefiting countless numbers of people. Often times I take time to examine my skills and abilities and consider how I can help someone else free of charge. This practice has been one of the best habits I have ever formed. Too often we rely on state and national agencies or even local organizations to make deposits into the lives of someone else. Each and every one of us can make a difference in the life of someone else by releasing our passion through volunteer acts.

I am enthusiastic when around the elderly because I value their wisdom. When I talk with them I feel as though I am getting a sneak peak at my future as I journey into their lives and realize that many of their life stories may one day be written in my life book. I enjoy working with them and listening to their life stories. When I am in their company I sing joyous songs and offer praises to them for making a difference in our world in their own special way. How wonderful it would be if more people shared this perspective. How much greater of an impact could be made if two people joined together to make a difference? Imagine a photographer and cosmetologist teaming up and volunteering their services at a senior residential community by taking memorable photographs and donating them as a gift? Opportunities for creative wellness activities are endless. Stretch your imagination and give back to your community enriching the lives of one person at a time.

Do you struggle to find structured activities when entertaining family and friends? Consider writing a composite of short stories about your parents or loved ones. Gather history about their birth and childhood and journey through their adolescent and young adult years. As you reminisce ask clarifying questions to make a complete story. Any family member can join in on this activity to make it more inclusive and personal for everyone. Simply make an outline beginning with the subject heading: Birth and Childhood. Ask as many questions as you would like to the interviewee to create a story that includes facts about their birth place, their parents and other pertinent memories. Ask the common How, What, When and Where questions to open a door way for more memories. Focus on sibling relationships, various losses and gains, holiday and vacation memories as well as personal stories of salvation. Include information about their educational, work and or military background. Explore past and present marital relationships and special friendships along the way. Delve into their dreams and aspirations, the best years of their life and celebrate their greatest accomplishments. You might ask about things they wish they may have done differently as this can ignite compassion and empathy that can enhance relations. Invite family members to submit questions of life events they would like to know more about from the interviewee. What an amazing way to grow and love together while creating a lasting memory for generations to come.

Another wellness activity I enjoy is hosting life goals parties that include family, close friends and associates. This is a time in your life where you can listen to the goals and dreams of others in order to jolt your own mind into thinking about what is important to you. Exchange ideas and strategies that will help you to overcome obstacles while embracing feedback that will empower you to think outside of the box. You will walk away from this type of gathering feeling renewed, empowered and confident that you are moving toward positive change and direction in your life.

Spirituality Survey to be taken by challenger

I support my church through regular attendance

1   2   3   4   5

I support my church through consistent tithing

1   2   3   4   5

I am responsive and reliable when called upon by church family

1   2   3   4   5

I visit or call the sick or shut-in

1   2   3   4   5

I spend time in prayer and bible study on a regular basis

1   2   3   4   5

I support missions outside of my local church

1   2   3   4   5

I am using my spiritual gifts and talents to help enhance worship and outreach in my local community

1   2   3   4   5

My counsel to others is not of my own personal opinion but derived from biblical teaching

1   2   3   4   5

The Parent Check Experience

I have come to realize that how I perceive myself as a parent effects how I view myself in other roles I fulfill. Therefore if I do not view myself as a confident and capable parent I am not likely going to feel very confident on the job or in other roles outside of my home environment. It is extremely important to me to view myself in a positive light.

Parent check is a series of thought provoking questions designed to help parents analyze their parenting ability through sentence completion or personal justification.

The purpose is not to rate yourself as a good or bad parent, rather, to challenge you to think about those things you appreciate about your parenting while looking at values and belief systems you may have adopted from your own parents. Ask yourself, what positive aspects of your parenting do you hope your own children will adopt and pass along to thier children? Are there values in your family you hope your child will embrace? What cyclic behaviors or attitudes are evident in your family history that you have not been able to change and what can you do to build courage and awareness in your children to aide them in breaking these negative patterns?

Parent Check challenges you to ask questions you may not typically ask yourself but afterwards will feel glad that you did. Take a minute to compose your thoughts and complete the sentences below. Notice there are plenty of lines for you to record your responses. I can not emphasize how beneficial it would be to ask yourself additional questions to stimulate your recollection. Think about what has happened in your life and what you had the power to control. Consider how these experiences shaped who you are today and how they inadvertently affect those who are closest to you. This is your journal so feel free to boast. Ask your self the standard "who, what, when, where and how did it turn out?" to trigger more expanded responses. As an incentive, give yourself a point range of 10 points for simply completing the journal exercise to 25 points for being thorough in your responses.

My greatest strength as a parent is

_____

_____

_____

_____

_____

_____

_____

_____

_____

_____

One thing I would like to improve about my parenting ability is

_____

_____

_____

_____

_____

_____

_____

_____

_____

_____

_____

_____

_____

_____

I plan to make these improvements

_____

_____

_____

_____

_____

_____

_____

_____

_____

_____

_____

_____

_____

When I think about my parents I really appreciate them for

_____

_____

_____

_____

_____

_____

_____

_____

_____

_____

_____

_____

_____

_____

Camella Jones

I feel my parenting style is similar to my own parents because

_____

_____

_____

_____

_____

_____

_____

_____

_____

_____

_____

_____

_____

As I think about my own parents, I finally understand why
they

_____

_____

_____

_____

_____

_____

_____

_____

_____

_____

_____

_____

_____

The most meaningful lesson I have taught my children is

_____

_____

_____

_____

_____

_____

_____

_____

_____

_____

_____

_____

As a parent it is important to me that my child(ren) know how I feel about

_____

_____

_____

_____

_____

_____

_____

_____

_____

_____

_____

_____

_____

_____

I have taken the foundation my parent(s) have laid before me and

_____

_____

_____

_____

_____

_____

_____

_____

_____

_____

_____

_____

_____

_____

I hope my child(ren) never forget the time we

_____

_____

_____

_____

_____

_____

_____

_____

_____

_____

_____

_____

_____

I want my children to be successful in life. It is important that

_____

_____

_____

_____

_____

_____

_____

_____

_____

_____

_____

_____

_____

For a while I was angry about

_____

_____

_____

_____

_____

_____

_____

_____

_____

_____

_____

_____

_____

_____

_____

I understand that one day I will die. My wishes

_____

_____

_____

_____

_____

_____

_____

_____

_____

_____

_____

_____

_____

The best piece of advice I can give to another parent

_____

_____

_____

_____

_____

_____

_____

_____

_____

_____

_____

_____

_____

Camella Jones

My childhood was a struggle at times

_____

_____

_____

_____

_____

_____

_____

_____

_____

_____

_____

_____

_____

It wouldn't hurt to admit and apologize to my child(ren) for

_____

_____

_____

_____

_____

_____

_____

_____

_____

_____

_____

_____

_____

_____

Camella Jones

I can laugh with my children about

_____

_____

_____

_____

_____

_____

_____

_____

_____

_____

_____

_____

_____

Enhancing family and marital relations through the Wellness Experience

These are only a few examples of countless questions you can ask yourself to began a journey toward improved self awareness about how your yesterday effects who you are today. Now that you have completed the exercises in the Wellness Activity Book I would encourage you to enhance your experience by sitting down with your loved one to discuss any insight you may have gained. Consider areas you have fallen short and explore actions you are willing to take in order to improve your life and relationships with others. You may find that the help of a professional counselor or perhaps spiritual guidance can be helpful throughout this process.

I encourage parents to keep an open line of communication with their children. Consider a family meeting at a designated time and location each week to capture "sparkling moments." Have your child write or state all of the good deeds they have performed over the course of the week. Regardless of how big or small the deed parents are encouraged to offer praise and esteem for the child's efforts. This practice will condition the child to look for opportunities to perform good deeds while parents begin developing a natural habit of recognizing and applauding their children. Do not be surprised if the child shifts the focus onto the parent and begins to offer praises for the good things you do. By all means savor the moment if this happens.

I can not tell you how many sparkling moments our family has captured after opening the doorway to our children. Within a short time unknown concerns and problems the children were dealing with were being brought up for discussion. As a result of their regular acknowledgment, I have seen an increased level of trust and confidence in them.

I want to warn you that if you have not been in a habit of sitting down and talking with your children without outside distractions you might prepare for the first few meetings to go slowly and perhaps feel somewhat awkward. Please stay focused and remember that once your child discovers that the intent of the family meetings are to recognize the good things they are doing they will soon take advantage of the safe environment and begin to share more of what is going on in their daily lives.

I strongly encourage couples to sit down together on a weekly basis and ask the question, "Are you happy?" It is such a wonderful feeling to know that my husband is willing to make adjustments or offer suggestions that could change the way that I feel. I believe both individuals in the marital relationship are obligated to do their part in ensuring the happiness of the other.

Keep in mind that the idea of asking the question, "Are you happy?" is not to make your spouse or mate feel responsible for your happiness, rather, to extend an invitation for each of you to be heard, share your views or feelings and even concerns about certain issues in your relationship. Just as children have sparkling moments that need to be high lighted, couples should reassure one another regularly and also capture happy moments in the marriage as this can be very encouraging. Before change can occur in your relationship both of you must identify what you are willing to do to increase the degree of happiness your spouse or mate feels. It's imperative that you make small commitments as change is a process. It can be very damaging to a relationship to have a promise made that is not kept. Consider this example of a wife that is unhappy because her husband 1) is not spending enough quality time with her 2) does not help with the household chores 3) watches too much television. The husband gets to choose which of the three problem areas he wants to work on and together you would agree on the possible solutions and reward for success in addressing a potentially disastrous situation.

Remember to keep things simple. It would be counterproductive for either of you to regret making any commitment toward change if doing so results in a feeling of torment. Time is needed to undo bad habits that have developed over the course of any relationship so be sure to celebrate small accomplishments in your journey to conscious change and spontaneous effect. The survey below is a great door opener for in depth discussion and potential problem solving as in the example discussed earlier. Talk about your responses and each should meditate on feedback in order to make commitments to move toward change resultant of your many new relational discoveries.

Couple's Survey

My spouse or mate views me as honest and trustworthy

1   2   3   4   5

My spouse or mate is certain of my love and believes that I will go to great lengths to ensure peace, harmony and happiness in our relationship

1   2   3   4   5

My spouse or mate feels we have open communication in our relationship and are able to talk through our issues

1   2   3   4   5

My spouse or mate feels that I support and respect their goals, dreams and feelings

1   2   3   4   5

My spouse or mate feels I am committed and willing to seek counseling if a clear indication from this survey suggests our relationship is at risk for breakdown

1   2   3   4   5

My spouse makes me laugh and feel good about myself

1   2   3   4   5

My spouse is compassionate and considerate of my needs

1   2   3   4   5

My spouse can depend on me for emotional, spiritual and financial support

1   2   3   4   5

My spouse shares the responsibility for rearing the children and balancing household responsibilities

1   2   3   4   5

I am not currently struggling with any issues or decisions that I have not discussed with my spouse or mate

1   2   3   4   5

Couple's Survey

My spouse or mate views me as honest and trustworthy

1   2   3   4   5

My spouse or mate is certain of my love and believes that I will go to great lengths to ensure peace, harmony and happiness in our relationship

1   2   3   4   5

My spouse or mate feels we have open communication in our relationship and are able to talk through our issues

1   2   3   4   5

My spouse or mate feels that I support and respect their goals, dreams and feelings

1   2   3   4   5

My spouse or mate feels I am committed and willing to seek counseling if a clear indication from this survey suggests our relationship is at risk for breakdown

1   2   3   4   5

My spouse makes me laugh and feel good about myself

1   2   3   4   5

My spouse is compassionate and considerate of my needs

1   2   3   4   5

My spouse can depend on me for emotional, spiritual and financial support

1   2   3   4   5

My spouse shares the responsibility for rearing the children and balancing household responsibilities

1   2   3   4   5

I am not currently struggling with any issues or decisions that I have not discussed with my spouse or mate

1   2   3   4   5

Couple's Survey

My spouse or mate views me as honest and trustworthy

1   2   3   4   5

My spouse or mate is certain of my love and believes that I will go to great lengths to ensure peace, harmony and happiness in our relationship

1   2   3   4   5

My spouse or mate feels we have open communication in our relationship and are able to talk through our issues

1   2   3   4   5

My spouse or mate feels that I support and respect their goals, dreams and feelings

1   2   3   4   5

My spouse or mate feels I am committed and willing to seek counseling if a clear indication from this survey suggests our relationship is at risk for breakdown

1   2   3   4   5

My spouse makes me laugh and feel good about myself

1   2   3   4   5

My spouse is compassionate and considerate of my needs

1   2   3   4   5

My spouse can depend on me for emotional, spiritual and financial support

1   2   3   4   5

My spouse shares the responsibility for rearing the children and balancing household responsibilities

1   2   3   4   5

I am not currently struggling with any issues or decisions that I have not discussed with my spouse or mate

1   2   3   4   5

Couple's Survey

My spouse or mate views me as honest and trustworthy

1   2   3   4   5

My spouse or mate is certain of my love and believes that I will go to great lengths to ensure peace, harmony and happiness in our relationship

1   2   3   4   5

My spouse or mate feels we have open communication in our relationship and are able to talk through our issues

1   2   3   4   5

My spouse or mate feels that I support and respect their goals, dreams and feelings

1   2   3   4   5

My spouse or mate feels I am committed and willing to seek counseling if a clear indication from this survey suggests our relationship is at risk for breakdown

1   2   3   4   5

My spouse makes me laugh and feel good about myself

1   2   3   4   5

My spouse is compassionate and considerate of my needs

1   2   3   4   5

My spouse can depend on me for emotional, spiritual and financial support

1   2   3   4   5

My spouse shares the responsibility for rearing the children and balancing household responsibilities

1   2   3   4   5

I am not currently struggling with any issues or decisions that I have not discussed with my spouse or mate

1   2   3   4   5

Camella Jones

Couple's Survey

My spouse or mate views me as honest and trustworthy

1   2   3   4   5

My spouse or mate is certain of my love and believes that I will go to great lengths to ensure peace, harmony and happiness in our relationship

1   2   3   4   5

My spouse or mate feels we have open communication in our relationship and are able to talk through our issues

1   2   3   4   5

My spouse or mate feels that I support and respect their goals, dreams and feelings

1   2   3   4   5

My spouse or mate feels I am committed and willing to seek counseling if a clear indication from this survey suggests our relationship is at risk for breakdown

1   2   3   4   5

My spouse makes me laugh and feel good about myself

1   2   3   4   5

My spouse is compassionate and considerate of my needs

1   2   3   4   5

My spouse can depend on me for emotional, spiritual and financial support

1   2   3   4   5

My spouse shares the responsibility for rearing the children and balancing household responsibilities

1   2   3   4   5

I am not currently struggling with any issues or decisions that I have not discussed with my spouse or mate

1   2   3   4   5

A word from the author about your Wellness Experience

It is my hope that The Wellness Activity book has helped you develop a sense of pride and confidence in the small things you do every day to contribute to an improved state of well-being. I encourage you to continue moving toward wellness by making these activities a natural part of your daily life and by inspiring others to join in this revolutionary fun new approach to preserving families and relationships.

The Daily Points Guide

Week 1

	Physical and Nutritional Health Category	Spiritual Health	Altruistic Category	Personal Category	Relaxation Category	Daily Combined Surveys Category
Sunday						
Monday						
Tuesday						
Wednesday						
Thursday						
Friday						
Saturday						
Total:						

Week 2

	Physical and Nutritional Health Category	Spiritual Health	Altruistic Category	Personal Category	Relaxation Category	Daily Combined Surveys Category
Sunday						
Monday						
Tuesday						
Wednesday						
Thursday						
Friday						
Saturday						
Total:						

Week 3

	Physical and Nutritional Health Category	Spiritual Health	Altruistic Category	Personal Category	Relaxation Category	Daily Combined Surveys Category
Sunday						
Monday						
Tuesday						
Wednesday						
Thursday						
Friday						
Saturday						
Total:						

Week 4

	Physical and Nutritional Health Category	Spiritual Health	Altruistic Category	Personal Category	Relaxation Category	Daily Combined Surveys Category
Sunday						
Monday						
Tuesday						
Wednesday						
Thursday						
Friday						
Saturday						
Total:						

The Daily Points Guide

Week 1

	Physical and Nutritional Health Category	Spiritual Health	Altruistic Category	Personal Category	Relaxation Category	Daily Combined Surveys Category
Sunday						
Monday						
Tuesday						
Wednesday						
Thursday						
Friday						
Saturday						
Total:						

Week 2

	Physical and Nutritional Health Category	Spiritual Health	Altruistic Category	Personal Category	Relaxation Category	Daily Combined Surveys Category
Sunday						
Monday						
Tuesday						
Wednesday						
Thursday						
Friday						
Saturday						
Total:						

Week 3

	Physical and Nutritional Health Category	Spiritual Health	Altruistic Category	Personal Category	Relaxation Category	Daily Combined Surveys Category
Sunday						
Monday						
Tuesday						
Wednesday						
Thursday						
Friday						
Saturday						
Total:						

Week 4

	Physical and Nutritional Health Category	Spiritual Health	Altruistic Category	Personal Category	Relaxation Category	Daily Combined Surveys Category
Sunday						
Monday						
Tuesday						
Wednesday						
Thursday						
Friday						
Saturday						
Total:						